DICTION II: THE PARADOX OF FAITH

DICTION II: THE PARADOX OF FAITH

A Dictionary of Benedictions

J. A. Gucci

CONTENTS

A NOTE ON READING

Diction II: The Paradox of Faith is an applied work of *Absolute Composition.* Each entry pairs a named article of faith with an observable phenomenon and a benediction. The article of faith appears as the title. The body of the poem presents a physical system, event, condition, or transformation drawn from the observable world. The benediction emerges from the behavior of that system.

The poems do not attempt to explain faith through doctrine, confession, symbolism, or belief. Instead, they place articles of faith in structural correspondence with observable phenomena. The relationship between faith and phenomenon is not allegorical. It is behavioral.

Readers approaching this volume may find it useful to ask: What is happening? What persists? What crosses the threshold? What returns? What remains hidden? The answers are not concealed. They are structural.

Interpretation remains possible, but structure comes first. Meaning follows arrangement.

Nothing here persuades.

It witnesses.

*"This book does not confess.
It contains."*

9

SECTION I — THE ARC OF FAITH

ANOINTING

Silver slither,

shimmering crescent
shadows

black
face—

hooting owls,
wavelets over burrows.

Benediction: Distance anoints.

COVENANT

Oil lamp on a hook
vibrating

cast iron
screech—

shattered chimney,
halo.

*Benediction: What burns in the dark remembers the
light.*

CREATION

Slip face slammed by a sand cloud—
sparkling dune.

Benediction: Let friction name the first light.

FAITH

Soft peeps
rapid chirps,

fox gaze—

fluffed and fanned
fluttering

wings—
paw prints.

Benediction: Leap—though the ground vanishes.

GRACE

Poised at a crossroad—

scoff,
chuckle—

dry crunching,
dust plume.

Benediction: Let motion outrun meaning.

OBEDIENCE

Leaps over falls
walls—stone
silt loam,

belly shakes
scrapes
white skin grates,

grunts and growls—
purr.

Benediction: Return, even if nothing waits.

REVELATION

Snowflake
alight on honeycomb.

*Benediction: See what repeats, and you will know what
endures.*

SACRIFICE

Willow
rooted in loam

dry
rooted in water—

catkins.

Benediction: Root where life remains.

SILENCE

Natant needle
drifting

widening ripple
still

pond.

Benediction: Let the ripple become the stillness.

THRESHOLD

Frost
clung to glass,

water hammers—

slithering beads
along the glass.

Benediction: Welcome what loosens its grip.

VEIL

Snowcapped peak
glimmering

cloud
drifting—

shrouded mountain.

Benediction: Not all hiding is absence.

SECTION II — THE CONSEQUENCES OF FAITH

AGAPE

Stylet and lancet
rammed into hide—

twitching
still curl.

Benediction: Give until giving stings.

COMPASSION

Brittle bored
log
slumped in loam,

seedlings—
canopy cedar.

Benediction: Become the ground.

DUST

Dust furling

squeezed
crushed

red glowing
blue—

giant.

Benediction: Let pressure reveal the light.

ECHO

Pitch fork
settled on the flylid—

aeolian hum.

Benediction: Let the song find you.

EXILE

Chalky

fresh water reed
rooted in marsh,

spotted.

Benediction: Remain what crossed over.

FAITHFULNESS

Drooping yellow
brown

seeping
soil

spearing—
purple shoots.

Benediction: Keep faith with the hidden root.

FALTER

Cracked lime,
dry creek bed

gurgling—

cascade.

Benediction: What disappears may still endure.

FRACTURE

Glimmering warm
muddy clay,

dusty matte
hexagons.

Benediction: What breaks may still belong.

HOPE

Shrunk liver,

flapping,
coursing

over water
open.

Benediction: Cross before the shore appears.

HUMILITY

Monks in joggers
chanting Dorian.

Benediction: Let the song need nothing.

INCARNATION

Rumbles

plate—rammed into plate—

summit.

Benediction: Let the unseen take form.

JUDGMENT

Streaking light beam—
scattered dots.

Benediction: To see is to divide.

MERCY

Sheets of rain,
dripping canopy.

Benediction: Let strength arrive gently.

PRAYER

Sun glinting pond
dwindling,

wet air
rising.

Benediction: Let your diminishing rise.

REDEMPTION

Burbling liquid rock
cool—

fireweed.

Benediction: Bloom where the fire passed.

RESURRECTION

Supple green
blue radiating,

crisp and curled
coiled inward,

rain—
unfurling

green
supple blue

radiating

Benediction: Life remembers its shape.

SALVATION

Milk eyes

undulating coil
chafed

rotting in loam—
Peace Lily.

Benediction: Leave behind what once protected you; it
was never you at all.

SCAR

Rolling rumbles,
flash-strike—

fresh pale wood,
charred seam.

Benediction: Let survival remain visible.

SIN

Root drop—

clung to weeping green
hollow willow.

Benediction: Root before you cling.

SUFFERING

Surge

thrusting upslope—
dune slumps.

Backwash

thrusting upslope—
slides.

Benediction: Advance despite the slide.

TEMPTATION

High river burst

banks,
splayed

stagnant.

Benediction: Not every expansion is freedom.

TIME

Summit
settled in silt

sunk
under seafloor

spewed
out of a throat—

summit.

Benediction: Return by another road.

TRANSCENDENCE

Stardust in a rib.

Benediction: Where the infinite enters bone, breathe.

VIGIL

Dead
twisted trunk

thriving
green needles.

Benediction: Keep faith with the living vein.

WITNESS

Footprints in mud
silt
stone.

Benediction: What remains still speaks.

AFTERWORD

Faith is often treated as a matter of belief.

This volume approaches it differently.

The entries in this book do not argue for faith,
defend faith, or describe personal faith. They
recover articles of faith from observable
phenomena. Each poem presents a physical system,
event, condition, or transformation. The title names
an article of faith. The benediction emerges from
the behavior of the phenomenon itself.

The result is neither doctrine nor metaphor.

It is correspondence.

A river leaves its banks. A fern unfurls. A mountain
vanishes behind cloud. A footprint hardens into
stone. The phenomena remain what they are.
Nothing is added to them. Nothing is taken away.
Yet through their behavior, structures appear.

Faith begins there.

Not in certainty.

In recognition.

The world speaks first.

The benediction follows.

COLOPHON

This volume was set in Palatino and composed using Apple Pages.

Diction II: The Paradox of Faith is the second volume of The Paradox Trilogy:

Feeling — Faith — Thought

Each entry pairs an article of faith with an observable phenomenon and a benediction derived from its behavior.

The poems were composed according to the principles of Absolute Composition.

Printed in the United States of America.

www.ingramcontent.com/pod-product-compliance
Lightning Source LLC
Chambersburg PA
CBHW020513160726
47991CB00007B/2932